MODERN COMMON SENSE

MODERN COMMON SENSE

PERSPECTIVES FOR AMERICAN VOTERS

INSIGHTS INTO

Your Fellow Americans

American Thinking

The Portrayal of America

American Political Parties

Payne Edwards

Modern Common Sense

By Payne Edwards

Published by EPK Neavitt MD

Printed by Createspace

ISBN: 1725134322

Book design by Payne Edwards

Table of Contents

Introduction

In the past, Americans relied on common sense to pass judgment on what they'd heard, read or watched, and openly credited common sense as the basis for deciding what to do. Today, we are being told that common sense is not enough. Modern society is much too complex; our ever-expanding knowledge is increasingly specialized. Issues are far too complicated; only nuanced deep thinkers can see the subtleties. It's better to leave the analysis of events and decision-making to the experts and put common sense aside.

America is a huge country with a highly diversified population. For decades, the social sciences have been constructing academic tools to decipher societal complexity and improve our understanding. Surely, social scientific approaches can supplement or even replace homespun common sense as a means for conducting assessments or making policy decisions.

Regrettably, this has not proven to be the case. The social sciences have saturated our schools and the media with a kind of mindless oversimplification of America. Unintentionally, they have created a paradigm that is more an impediment to thinking than an aid to enlightenment. They have fostered various narratives of conventional wisdom that have caused confusion, bred misunderstanding and created divisive politics.

I think that Americans need to reconsider the paradigm. This book is meant to be a guide. It breaks down today's America into some of its component parts and puts them in perspective. The chapters are intended to give Americans a more realistic sense of themselves and their country.

The first three chapters reexamine your fellow Americans: the people, their values and their diversity. Chapter one puts the population in perspective: how many Americans there are in a way that makes the large number tangible. Then, it examines the work that they do: the career fields, professions and types of employment. Chapter two takes a fresh look at American values and reveals how they have evolved to become a set of beliefs that Americans generally hold in common. Chapter three addresses the country's diversity. Not the buzz-word term that is bandied about, but rather a bird's eye view of the diversity found in communities across the country.

The fourth chapter is ambitious and unconventional. In "The American Intellect," it describes how Americans think. The relatively new fields of behavioral economics and analysis of expert judgment have shown that the decisions which people make may be the result of honest, open thinking, biased or faulty thinking, or, in some cases, with no real thinking at all. Yet, individuals make decisions convinced that they have appropriately thought things through. Most people rely on common sense, either unconsciously or deliberately. But a sizeable number of Americans have been educated to think beyond common sense. In the course of completing a college degree, they develop different approaches to thinking that influence the way they evaluate the world around them, affects the beliefs they adopt and influences the decisions they make.

The next three chapters comprise what I call "The American Portrayal:" how is America and how are Americans described and defined, and by whom. America is portrayed in elementary and secondary schools, on college campuses, and in the dominant media, including print, broadcast and entertainment. These institutions share common characteristics that play a significant role in crafting the portrayal. The number of people who control the institutions is a small, and in some instances, minuscule number. They are cloistered in settings that are essentially estranged from those where most Americans live and work. And the few people in charge are similarly college educated and mostly think alike.

On a daily basis, what Americans think about things is background noise that may slowly influence economic markets and the culture over time. But on Election Day, what they think decides a political contest. It is the rare day when how Americans think results in one person being elected to office for two, four or six years. Two chapters look at elections from different vantage points: the parties and the voters. It discusses how the political parties define themselves and seek to divide Americans to garner their votes.

This analysis of modern America is meant to illuminate and educate, not to suggest new policies. That said, in a way, it points to an indirect solution: a more informed, aware and independent-thinking electorate. A few words of motivation to become a savvier consumer of information and a more engaged voter are offered in conclusion.

Individual Americans

To understand America, you need to know your fellow citizens. There are about 330 million Americans. About 155 million are active in the workforce. But it is hard to make sense of so many people. Large numbers are simply not intuitive. About the only time that we can process numbers in a meaningful way is when dealing with money. We can attach real things to dollar amounts: $10,000 can pay for a great vacation; $100,000 a year provides a comfortable living, some luxuries, and the chance to build a nest egg; a million opens many more doors. Beyond money, large numbers lose relevance. It is exceptionally difficult to comprehend a million things, such as people. Instead, the media assign individuals to demographic groups because they find it easier to deal with a handful of categories. Yet, despite decades of conditioning the public to look at America as a collection of groups, the fact remains that we interact with one another as individuals, not as group members.

To reconsider the notion that most Americans think along similar lines, that they share what has been popularly termed 'common ground,' you need to think about the American people in new and different ways to break free from the media shorthand. First, envision Americans as individuals.

You need to conceptualize the population beyond being a large, abstract number, something that doesn't lend itself to an image that your brain can process. By using your imagination and thinking hard, however, you can see large numbers in your mind's eye. Read the following paragraphs slowly. Stop and think after reading each one until you visualize the description.

You are in the stands of a football stadium, a few seats up on the fifty yard line.

A marching band begins to take the field. The first element is arrayed ten across, in ten ranks. A cohort of one hundred marches onto the field.

A similar set marches in to the left of the first.

Eight more cohorts take their place behind the two in front.

On either side of the fifty yard line, from sideline to sideline, the band is now one thousand. From your seat on the fifty yard line, you can see one thousand people.

It is not that difficult to stretch an image of one thousand to a million and still retain a workable sense of proportion. Keep your image of one thousand in mind.

Now picture the huge oval stands in the Los Angeles Coliseum.

Your one thousand (the band on the field) slowly enters the stadium and sits together in one section. A second group does the same, followed by another, and so on. We film them taking their seats, one after the other, until the stadium is full.

Then we condense the film to a time-lapse video so that each one thousand pops into their seats every second.

The one hundred second long video reveals how sets of one thousand have become a crowd of one-hundred thousand.

Now we pretend that the Coliseum is magically circled by nine other Coliseums. Looking down on them from a helicopter, we see one million.

Please pause here for a moment. Replay the video of the filling Coliseum in your mind's eye. Revisualize the hundreds and the thousands as they finally fill the stands. Close your eyes if it helps.

To further visualize the proportions, imagine that your first one thousand are all wearing red hats while everyone else is wearing white. We can spot your one thousand quite easily, not really a speck in a sea of white, but more like a little island. And then suppose that one of your thousand replaces the red hat with a white one. Surrounded by those in red, that person is one in a thousand; and amidst everyone in all ten Coliseums, one in a million.

We are bombarded today with pronouncements about what Americans want, what they believe, and who they support. Polls somehow magically capture the sentiments of many millions of people. I won't dig into the validity of polls and polling, but I will delve into the arena of commonly held sentiments and beliefs. And this requires parsing some numbers and providing proportion, perspective and context.

Hopefully being able to picture large numbers of Americans, and to see them as a collection of individuals, it's time to view them a second way by examining the 155 million in the workforce.

Who is doing what? To try to make sense of this, let's explore a microcosm of the employed. Consider a little county with one town. It is home to 330 people. Many don't work at all. They include the children, the elderly, the disabled and some parents. A little over half work, 155 full time and 35 part-time. I'll stipulate that the county workforce reflects the nation-wide workforce as of 2017. For example, there were 17,401,000 employed nationally in health care; I've reduced the approximately 17 million nationally to 17 individuals in the county. The table below shows what kind of work is done by the full-time employees of this little county.

Private Sector and Education (Full Time Employees only)

Health Care	17	Transportation	7
Retail Trade	17	Business Services	7
Manufacturing	15	Wholesale Trade	4
Education	14	Real Estate	3
Tech-Pro Services	12	Information	3
Restaurant/Hotel	11	Social Assistance	3
Construction	11	Arts, Entertainment, Rec.	3
Trade-Pro Services	7	Agriculture	3
Finance	7	Energy	2
		Sub Total: 146	

Government

Local	3	State	2
Federal	2	Defense	2
		Total: 155	

This is a numerical metaphor for the United States. Three hundred thirty represents the total population; 155 represent the millions who are employed full time. Please go back and look at the table, and ponder how many are doing what kind of work.

We will reach some remarkable contrasts later in terms of what average people are doing versus what you are told, shown, or led to believe. But I am getting ahead of myself.

These categories are broad, but telling[1]. A third of all employees work in two areas: health care and retail trade. The three fields I characterize as hands-on work (manufacturing, restaurants and construction) make up well over another third. Education is a major employer and includes teachers, professors, administrators and a large number of supporting personnel. Tech-Pro is shorthand for technical and professional fields, including computer, legal, accounting, design and engineering services. Trade-Pro services include salons, auto repair, plumbers and such. Business services provide building maintenance, landscaping, employment services, and security. Half of social assistance is child care and the other half various social workers. Energy employs those who provide utilities and those who drill for oil and gas. We'll examine the Information and Arts/Entertainment/Recreation categories in greater detail later. But here is a teaser on them. Within the information category we find essentially the entire 'main-stream' media: newspapers, magazines, books, radio, television and the movies. Arts, entertainment and recreation are dominated by amusements, gambling, spectator sports, museums and the performing arts. Perhaps it is some kind of indicator that organizations that compile employment statistics include all the popular media into a category entitled Information.

The table separates government employees from those in the private sector and education. The categories capture the kind of work done by employees, what I'll call their field of work. They do not indicate what employs them. The field of education illustrates this distinction. Most in this field are paid by state and local governments. Similarly, a sizable portion of those in the field of health care are local, state or federal employees. The government categories reflect those fields that are uniquely functions of government. National defense is the most obvious example. Other fields include police, fire fighting, the judicial system, jails and prisons, natural resources and environmental protection and other governmental regulatory agencies, the state department and, of course, revenue collection.

Consider for a moment what barely makes the list. One is actually quite remarkable. Among the three in agriculture, two would be farmers and one would be a rancher. This modern little county reveals that what used to employ a majority of Americans, farming, barely figures into the main fields of work. Meanwhile, the number of people doing things for other people, mostly providing services to one another, has grown tremendously. They interact with one another, sometimes being the service provider, sometimes a supplier to the provider or seller, and sometimes as the customer.

To describe U.S. fields of employment, I've used the little county to paint a picture of the economy as a whole. In keeping with the first part of this piece, I've chosen to humanize nationwide employment with numbers rather than percentages. Now let's visualize it.

Typically, one of the theaters in your local multiplex movie house seats two hundred people. It is just the right size to hold all the people of the little county who work full time. You get there early and watch as your fellow movie-goers fill the seats. If you're a lawyer in town, a teller at the bank or a stylist at the salon, you'd know some of them. If you work at the grocery store or in the hospital emergency room, you'd recognize more than a few. If you work at the assembly plant, you might choose to sit (or avoid sitting) next to your supervisor. You might even recognize the town bus driver, the electric company meter reader, one or two of your kid's teachers, and the clerk at the hardware store. You'd be surrounded by people who spend most of their day at work, who take some time to tend to their personal affairs and then manage to squeeze in a couple of hours being entertained, like at the movies. You're pretty much the same as the others in the crowd. As the auditorium lights dim and the movie begins, you're happy to be there. And you mind your manners so as not to disturb the happiness of others.

Why go through the effort to look at your fellow Americans in these ways? Why is it necessary to have a handle on how many of us there are and what occupies our time?

We've left the movie theater. The next day, you take a seat in the stands at one of the Coliseums and scan your fellow attendees. Most of the crowd is a blur of color and shapes, but some of the people sitting in nearby seats are clearly distinguishable as real human beings. Most exchange pleasantries with others in nearby seats and often extend them courtesies. Some even share smirks when an excited fan makes something of a scene. Everyone is there to enjoy the game and is mindful to see that they don't upset the positive mood.

Almost all of the fans earn a living in the private sector or education in the fields of work listed in the table. Somewhere in the stands there may be someone from a small subset of one of the fields. There may be a logger or a fisherman, a veterinarian, perhaps even a ballet dancer, a furniture maker or a craft beer brewer. On a rare occasion, we may spot a regional celebrity, a state delegate or the metro news weatherman. In a truly rare happenstance, we might see Oprah Winfrey, Tiger Woods or Tom Cruise.

Barely visible are the cameras televising the action on the field. High above in the press box, a handful of reporters are covering the game, a couple from newspapers, a radio announcer, and the television play by play broadcaster and the color commentator. Nationwide, the television audience could fill twenty more coliseums, except there wouldn't be twenty more press boxes; they'd be listening to those reporting from the game.

The focus of the people in the stands and those in front of a television is on a mere handful of people: the twenty-some players on the field who are doing something and the voices that are providing the narration. The vast majority of Americans are spectators.

The concept of Americans as spectators is very important. Even though they are all players in the game of life in their communities and workplaces, they rely on the daily newspaper, the local newscast and the national networks to follow events outside their immediate environment. In a sports event, the game is well-defined. The players are obvious, the rules well known and the results generally indisputable. It doesn't really matter that millions may be watching what camera angles a few producers decide to use in televising it, nor does it much matter what the announcers are saying. Other games of life, however, are not so clear-cut, leaving the media and educators tremendous latitude to tell us what millions of Americans are doing and what they are thinking.

American Values

When people advocate for policies, they frequently reference American values. Regrettably, the values often cited by politicians and interest group spokesmen are little more than labels or jargon, such as social justice, equality or limited government. But the American culture does in fact reflect attitudes, behaviors and desires that comprise what could collectively be called American values. When separated from ideology and policy advocacy, a majority of Americans, and in some cases almost all, hold the same or similar values.

Since its founding, the Washington International Center has introduced visitors to life in the United States. In examining the values of those from foreign cultures, the Center has learned how the American culture is markedly different than others, and why visitors are often mystified by how Americans treat one another and how they behave. In seeking to explain to visitors what drives Americans to act the way they do, the Center identified thirteen values that are uniquely American. In "The Values Americans Live By," L. Robert Kohls opens his piece with this insightful passage.

> Most Americans would have a difficult time telling you, specifically, what the values are that Americans live by. They have never given the matter much thought. Even if Americans had considered this question, they would probably, in the end, decide not to answer in terms of a definitive list of values. The reason for this is itself one very American value – their belief that every individual is so

unique that the same list of values could never be applied to all, or even most, of their fellow citizens[2].

As a national blend of immigrants and Indian tribes, each coming from their own culture, we have all adopted values that make the American culture unique, different from that of other parts of the world, sometimes very different. This is quite remarkable, that over time, people from varied cultures adopt a core set of values that are widely accepted. The stunning thing about the list of American values is that you'd be hard pressed to find a neighbor, co-worker or relative who would disavow any of them.

American values cross over several definitions of the word. Values can be attitudes, standards of behavior or desires. They may also be what people believe is important, worthwhile or useful. You need to approach this listing with an open mind. So inundated with buzz-words and slogans, we have been conditioned to project our own definition onto the values cited by others, rather than demand that they clearly define them. Each value in the list is given a title, hopefully one that accurately depicts its full definition.

I have expanded and extrapolated the thirteen values identified by Mr. Kohls into twenty-one and then grouped them in categories. This is meant to put them in context, to shed light on their origin and explain their development. Values can and do change with time and circumstances. As Mr. Kohls explained, Americans rarely consider their shared values, believing that a nation of individuals in a free society adopt their own personal set. And they do, of course. But the cultural phenomenon of the United States is that most individuals adopt similar ones.

The categories are legacy, modern and unique.

Legacy Values

Legacy values arose from the Declaration of Independence. In part, they were written into the Constitution and the Bill of Rights. They continued to develop during our early history when a mix of people governed by Constitutions and representative democracies, state and federal, spread westward.

Effective and responsive government operating within defined boundaries. Americans believe in government of, by and for the people, whether it is in their county, city, state or federal. They insist on government that is structured and empowered in written charters, so it is transparent and accountable.

Realistic and effective civil and criminal justice. Americans know that they will have disagreements and there will always be criminals. Against this reality, they demand effective mechanisms and institutions to justly handle civil disputes and lawbreakers.

Equality of opportunity. This bedrock of American values is enshrined in the preamble to the Declaration of Independence as the unalienable rights of life, liberty and the pursuit of happiness. Every person has an equal right to opportunity, without exception and without impediment.

Personal control. Americans believe that they are the master of their fate. They believe that with hard work, applied knowledge and sometimes through teamwork, they can conquer any challenge.

Free enterprise. Unless there is an obvious and compelling necessity for government regulation, Americans believe that a free market will provide better goods and services at reasonable prices than any other economic construct.

Practicality. Good old American ingenuity is more than a maxim; it reflects the idea that a rational, thoughtful and realistic approach to matters can produce results.

Directness and Honesty. Nuance may be the path to intellectual enlightenment, but it finds no place in the real world of industry and commerce. Business, which engages all but a sliver of the population, runs on integrity, trust and transparency. Americans realize that they must be direct and honest to gain and keep customers.

Obligation to others. When you agree to charter a government empowered by "we the people," it becomes a compact among its constituents. Americans may be individualists, but they are also imbued with a commitment beyond their immediate friends and family; they have realized that it is necessary to support the larger community.

Free primary and secondary education. Some may wonder how this is a value. It is one of the first commitments that free Americans made to one another. It is written into some state constitutions. It is also a reflection of their realization that to govern themselves, the people must be educated to understand the structure, rules and physical realities that govern human societies.

Modern Values

Modern values grew out of the need to protect legacy values in a modernizing, industrial society.

Regulated monopolies and anti-trust. As citizens, Americans realized that free markets and unregulated commerce, as crucial as they were to individual liberty and economic freedom, could produce anomalies. The natural ambition and enterprise of motivated people could create great things, but could also lead to conglomerations and manipulation of markets. They instructed their representatives to implement appropriate regulations to keep the playing field level.

Regulated financial markets. Financial markets and central banks are considered a necessary evil by many Americans. A ready, unfettered supply of capital is vital to expand free markets and to provide loans for operating expenses. But players in the money markets are merely there to make more money, not necessarily to create anything or to promote a sound economy. Since the days of Hamilton and Jefferson there has been contentious debate and different systems for controlling and issuing notes and specie. With the adoption of the Federal Reserve System in 1913, the central bank structure has found acceptance and proven to be effective, both for serving the free market, and for protecting the value of citizens' assets. Yet the money markets and financial derivatives markets are still held with suspicion. Americans value the need to regulate them strictly.

Progressive Taxation. First introduced with the ratification of the sixteenth amendment in 1913, the income tax was highly progressive. There were seven brackets, the first from zero to $20,000 and the seventh beginning at $500,000, which in today's dollars is around $450,000 and $11,500,000 respectively. The tax rates stepped up from one to seven percent. With a standard exemption of $3,000 and $4,000, the majority of Americans paid no income tax. To finance World War I, the number of brackets grew to twenty-one and the rates went up dramatically. For incomes over $100,000, the rate was 31%, and for incomes above $2,000,000, the rate was 67%. Brackets and rates since then have been adjusted, but the income tax remains highly progressive. Most communities also tax wealth on a quasi progressive basis by levying property taxes based on the appraised value of land holdings. Some communities even provide property tax exemptions for the elderly and disabled. Americans accept and value the idea that those who have achieved freedom-based financial success should pay more taxes.

Social Security and Medicare. Controversial initiatives of the New Deal, they gained acceptance as a way to care for the elderly and the very poor. Much of the acceptance was because it was structured in ways that reflected legacy values. It seemed practical, in that it was essentially a savings account, albeit a forced one. It was honestly and transparently structured. And it was consistent with Americans' sense of owing an obligation to others.

Unemployment Insurance. Many states had implemented unemployment insurance programs early in the twentieth century, at the behest of the people. Americans recognize that a free market system, although the best path to prosperity for all, is, by necessity, constantly adjusting to change and unexpected circumstances. Through no fault of their own, an industrializing free market results in people losing their jobs. These programs, much like Social Security, were broadly accepted because they were consistent with legacy values.

Clean environment. Americans insist on a clean environment, and frequently are unmindful of how successful they have been. From national parks, to limiting dangerous air pollution, to implementing standards and regulation for clean lakes and rivers, America is the envy of the world.

Immigration. Americans know that their country has been a blend of immigrants and Native Americans from the time of the earliest English and Spanish settlements. Their families came here to enjoy American freedom and to share in American prosperity and opportunity, and that required a healthy degree of assimilation. The most vocal advocates on the subject today are those who have recently arrived, taken the tests, and enthusiastically adopted American values. Americans welcome immigration, even though they have legitimate disagreements over the pace and the policies that apply to individual immigrants.

Unique Values

Unique values have developed through practice, usage and shared experiences as a result of national and international events, societal dynamics and technological change.

Community standards. Americans believe they should have a say in how their neighborhoods look and how people should behave with respect to their neighbors. They'll treat this gently, until the behavior of others become egregious. It is a value, nonetheless, that motivates people to action.

Charities and Civic Organizations. Alexis de Tocqueville was the first to observe Americans' unique penchant to form civic groups for social, educational or charitable causes. It is a reflection of the belief in self-reliance. Yet it is not the self-reliance of individualism. People know that groups are a vital asset for achieving positive outcomes for a community. Voluntary associations are an effective way to promote good works for the common good while preserving and protecting individual freedom, thereby avoiding government involvement.

Informality. Americans believe that pretensions are a symptom of hierarchy; of the imposition of a class structure. They reject it by being informal. It may be a stretch to call it a value, but it does set America apart from most other cultures which insist on formality across defined and often rigid class social structures.

Mutual respect. American's demand that people treat one another with respect. As with informality, it is a commitment to an egalitarian culture. Only in America could the noun disrespect be turned into the verb, "dissed," or, as a reflection of informality, simply "dis."

Accepting and expecting change. Americans embrace change; it is necessary for improvement and progress. It may seem odd to call this acceptance an American value. But when compared to other cultures, many of which fear and avoid change, it can be seen that this attitude strongly influences the dynamics of American society.

I assert that a sizeable majority of Americans would associate themselves and their friends and families with these statements. In making the claim that polarization among Americans is greatly exaggerated, the core of the argument must prove that there is far more agreement and far less division than others claim. I believe that this widely held set of values offers evidence that this is the case. To be sure, people will agree with each of the values to varying degrees. But, taken as a set, they provide a commonality, a glue that binds Americans together, a cultural foundation for unity, shared goals and mutual trust.

American Diversity

Recently in America, the word diversity has been tossed about so as to become meaningless. But diversity is in fact nothing more than a descriptor of the variety found within something. When examining a rain forest, for example, we note the wide diversity of flora and fauna. When examining a country's diversity, a first step is to define the terms. Commonly, demographic categories are used. This is unfortunate, because it actually confuses clumps with true diversity.

By almost any measure, America is as diverse as any country in the world. Putting aside the population, consider the tangibles. America's geography and topography is remarkably varied. The landmass is predominantly surrounded by oceans. It borders but two other countries, and Canada's is a porous line of demarcation that barely separates the two peoples economically, and to a considerable degree, culturally. From mountains and glaciers, to expansive fertile plains, across deserts and swamps, and verdant hills and arid flats, the people make their homes in a myriad of ways within disparate communities. The climates vary from tropical to temperate to cold, from permanent snow pack to far from ever freezing.

The economy includes almost every market sector and kind of enterprise, resulting in a workforce diversified in skills, knowledge and experience across many fields. The people live in cities, large and small, in towns, even villages, and isolated rural areas. They move freely and often among these communities, often temporarily or periodically, and maintain close family ties with others in different states, cities and towns. America, physically, can't be other than diverse.

Spores grow within a Petri dish, taking nutrients from their unique culture. Similarly, Americans adapt and grow within America's unique culture, the customs, practices and beliefs of its people. It develops partly as a result of the diverse physical environments they inhabit, but as importantly, it is molded by communities, congregations of individuals who may come from different places but who are dedicated American-style liberty and equality.

The natural and geophysical diversity of the country plays a role in spawning unique aspects of American culture that are reflected in some common American values. The fifty states are endowed with abundant natural resources. American agriculture is the envy of the world, with expanses of rich, tillable soil, an agreeable climate, and abundant rainfall. One aspect of American diversity is overlooked: natural disasters. The climate that brings moisture and wallows in the vagaries of the jet stream plague America with tornadoes; about seventy-five percent of all of the world's tornadoes touch ground in the United States. The advantage of having oceans off its coasts also allows landfall for hurricanes. Wedged between the tropics and the semi-temperate zones, low pressure systems generate violent storms. And then there are the earthquakes, the sinkholes, the wildfires and even erupting volcanoes. The natural violence visited upon the United States is not the norm around the world. America's unfortunate natural circumstances are shared by a relatively small number of other countries. These include Japan (earthquakes, volcanoes and typhoons), Bangladesh (typhoons, floods and storms), Scotland (horrendous storms) and Russia (so vast that most of the weather violence is rarely recorded).

Freedom gives Americans the latitude to deal with disasters. The bad brings Americans together to help one another to contend with it. The local devastation of these events belies the idea that a central government, rather than the elbow grease of the neighbors, can restore the community or help the afflicted. Also, the violent weather reminds Americans that they are vulnerable and turmoil could come any day.

When first confronted with this violent aspect of the nature of the United States, new arrivals are often stunned at the reaction. Then, they witness how people respond. Soon they join in, and look to themselves and their neighbors, and realize that politician promises and government agents are often too late, too out of touch, and too distracted to meet the obvious needs. Family, friends and neighbors do the work, and notice that the newscasters dramatically cover the destruction and the victimization but then ignore the reconstruction. They groan at the politicians who describe how they celebrate the American spirit in the face of calamity while having not a clue as to what actually animates that spirit. They become perplexed when the editorial page and opinion writers try to blame a feckless or inadequately resourced government for the mess. Others get really annoyed when advocacy groups exploit the misery to promote the need for drastic steps to combat climate change, some even going so far as to blame those affected by the storm for not doing enough to stop using oil and gas.

America began and continues to be a blend of immigrants and Indian tribes. When diversity among the population is explained, it is wedged into broad, and essentially useless, census-based categories: white, black, Hispanic, Asian-American, etc. It's beyond riotously funny that in an age when a simple binary distinction, gender, is parsed into a dozen or more identities, the measure of the diversity of Americans remains confined to a handful of categories. This works for some sociologists and area studies professors, but in terms of seeing how a diverse population makes self-governance work, it is entirely counter-productive.

The categories themselves are at best superficial, if not downright silly. White (skin color), black (skin color), Hispanic (speaks Spanish?), Native American (since when?), Asian-American (as if Asian countries have a common culture). Still, the professors, pundits and pollsters tell us that Americans think and act based on arbitrary people categories. It's beyond absurd.

The important diversity in America is not the ethnic or geographical origin of its immigrants. After a generation or two, and often within a generation, that distinction is washed away. The diversity that drives the American culture is the plethora of communities that coexist. Some communities are geographical, most often areas in which one or two economic activities dominate. Some are social communities, groups woven together by shared ways of thinking, be they religious, political, social or intellectual. There are work-related communities, people drawn together by how they earn a living, be they farmers, teachers, lawyers or manufacturers. And there are common-interest communities, people stitched together by pursuits and activities, such as sailors, bikers, coin collectors and music-lovers. These communities don't care what census category its members fall into. Most, in fact, take steps to ensure that it doesn't matter.

Media outlets, political consultants and social studies academics have done more to advance the notion of a divided America by applying these broad demographic categories. They are in fact less than meaningless. Computer programmers understand the importance of accurate data, or perhaps more correctly, the dangers of inaccurate data, whereby garbage in leads to garbage out. So it is with news reporting, polling and social studies that attempt to draw conclusions from demographic data that is specious.

Consider "Asian-American." This category includes southern Chinese immigrants from the 1850's, Japanese immigrants from the 1920's, Vietnamese from the 1970's, Koreans from any decade, Pakistanis, Indians, Burmese, Thais, Indonesians, let alone Filipino's, Chinese from Taiwan, and Russians from East Siberia. People from these regions are as different as Irish-, Italian-, German-, Polish- or Greek-Americans are from one another, but the differences are lost in the clumping.

Then there is the Hispanic category. Apparently, all Mexicans are Hispanics, whether they are native Mexicans, descendents of Spanish, Portuguese or other European immigrants, or those whose ancestors were forced into the country as slaves. And they are clumped together with native Peruvians and Colombians, or immigrants thereto, and Argentineans, even though many of them are European immigrants, and, of course, Cubans, even though each of these countries and the people who inhabit them are as different from one another as their Asian counterparts. And what of Brazilians – they speak Portuguese. Then, visit Spain and try telling a local that you know what they're thinking, since they are Hispanic.

Perhaps the most regrettable of all is African-American. A continent almost the size of the U.S., Mexico and South America combined, Africa has an incredibly diverse population with a nearly countless number of different tribes, communities and histories. Our diversity would in fact be much richer if Americans of African descent were hyphenated Americans like those from Europe or Asia. To identify a few, there would be Ashanti, Berber, Dinka, Maasai, San, Tutsi and Zulu-Americans; even Pygmie-Americans.

Finally, there are "whites." The pale and pink ones, the tawny and olive skinned ones, and the white Japanese and steppe bleached Asians. The only likeness that they share is some absence of skin pigment. Silver blonde Nordics and black-maned Irish; ruddy faced Welsh and auburn tinged Normands; round faced Dutchmen;

stocky central Europeans and Russians; tanned Greeks, Turks and Lebanese. All white, kind of, but all quite different. And yet the professors in the university will tell you that they are somehow all alike.

This needless categorization fits neatly in the mind of comparative thinkers (comparative and other thinking are described in the next chapter). It provides for simple tabulation to make comparisons. Ironically, it leads its primary users in the social sciences to reach conclusions that are at best misleading, or at worst, dead wrong. It skews news reporting. Stories are written with the assumption that these few demographic groups agree with other group members on most issues. Most importantly, it debases American politics. Political campaigns degenerate into pandering to supposedly viable groups. The thorny, legitimate issues involved in adapting self-governance to modern developments and societal realities, the governmental approach to enhancing the general welfare are ignored. It even infects representative government. The American system is structured to be geographically representative. Districts and states may have different economies, different concerns and unique communities whose general interests are served by Representatives and Senators. Yet, the Congress is now organized in caucuses that represent groups as much, if not more than states or districts.

America is inherently and naturally diverse. Defining diversity as a measure of group representation within enterprises and institutions is a false and arbitrary measure.

Americans are more than comfortable with the diversity that surrounds them. The middle-eastern shop owner, the Korean hair dresser, the Pakistani doctor, the northern European nanny and the Russian technologist are stereotypes. The fact is that new immigrants blend into various communities, whether they are professional, geographical or interest-based. In doing so, they quickly begin to adopt American values.

To know and understand your fellow Americans it is very important to stop looking at them as groups. They are, instead, unique individuals. They live in different communities, work in different fields and engage in different pursuits. They have also learned to work together in lieu of their differences. They share much more in common than is portrayed by our educators, our campus social and area studies teachers, and the media. Having to work with one another within a free enterprise system and with respect for a healthy system of laws and rules, Americans have developed common values.

Americans act and behave as a result of their individual surroundings – the influence of work and community, and in keeping with their values. They also decide to act and behave because each one of them looks at things in different ways, and they think differently. Although to this point the emphasis has been on individuals and away from generalization, I believe that the process of human thinking can be explained with a reasonable degree of fidelity by making some general observations. In this way, perhaps we can gain a better understanding of how people form their opinions and make their decisions in a media-influenced society.

The American Intellect

In today's common usage, the word intellect often carries the connotation of an intellectual, a person who is said to possess superior reasoning powers. In what follows, the broader definition of the word is the subject. It is the first of three definitions found in my Webster's New World dictionary: the ability to reason or understand or to perceive relationships, differences, etc.; power of thought and mind. The intellect is the engine for making assessments, taking courses of action and passing judgment. It is the counter-balance to the other thing that can drive behavior: feelings.

In recent decades, behavioral economists have been learning that the drivers of human decision-making are much more dynamic than simple reasoning, than thinking things through in a deliberate, logical manner. Your intellect engine is frequently avoided, ignored or overruled by your feelings. In some respects, human behavior can be viewed as the result of an internal struggle between a person's feelings and intellect. Picture it like the cartoon depiction of our internal struggle between doing good and doing bad, between the little devil hovering over one side of our head and the little angel over the other. Only this struggle, metaphorically, might be drawn as a tussle between our head and our heart, or as an argument between Star Trek's Mr. Spock and Dr. McCoy. Yet, at some point, a person decides which side to take. Most often, the decisions are the result of a deliberate, conscious effort. They are made by thinking rather than by succumbing to feelings.

I suggest that the way people think is strongly influenced by their education. This is distinct from what they learn, the extent to which they master various subjects, or even the breadth of their knowledge base. The way of thinking is affected by the level of education reached. And for those who attend college, the field of study profoundly impacts their mode of thinking.

Pollsters routinely categorize people by their level of education. We don't ask why or how the level of education is relevant to a person's decisions, motivations or opinions. Perhaps we should. Is it correct to assume that with more education, people gain knowledge about this fantastically complex world we live in and are therefore better equipped to think through the issues of the day? In my experience, people exercise common sense regardless of their level of education. And often, those without college degrees display as much if not more than their college-educated counterparts.

Common sense is the time-honored term for practical human thinking. Webster's dictionary defines common sense as "ordinary good sense or sound practical knowledge." It is a mysterious phenomenon of human nature, a special combination of how people feel, how they sense their environment, and how they assess things based on what they know. Applying common sense, people draw on intuition and experience to evaluate what they see or hear. By their middle or late teens, most people have developed a healthy degree of common sense. That is why in most states people can drive or consent to marriage at sixteen and vote at eighteen.

Beyond common sense, thinking is described as critical, analytical or creative. Creative thinking is the source of new and innovative ideas, and is another mystery of the human mind. Analytical thinking is a way to separate a whole into its parts and understand the relationships through a logical sequence of steps. Critical thinking is more esoteric. It is what leads someone to adopt a viewpoint or to take a certain action. Summarizing the definition that

Edward Glaser offered in 1941[3], critical thinking is a persistent examination of all relevant evidence that leads to particular conclusions by recognizing unstated assumptions, using accurate language, and recognizing the existence or non-existence of relationships. The critical thinker tests the conclusions against ones that others have reached. Common sense is the starting point for critical thinking.

A sound general education is essential to developing critical thinking skills. It provides the practical knowledge that is its basis. Equally importantly, young people must be schooled in how to think critically. Classroom teachers are important, but so are parents, relatives and close family friends. Properly taught the general knowledge of their cultural and economic environment, even illiterate people can critically think things through.

College students are immersed in approaches to thinking that are commensurate with their field of study. One approach is geared to prepare students to become effective in a given career. Another provides the intellectual underpinnings to advance in a particular field. A third approach develops critical thinking. I label these three approaches as methodical thinking, comparative thinking and critical thinking.

Around 1.8 million Bachelor degrees are awarded every year according to the Department of Education Center for Education Statistics[4]. It lists thirty-two fields of study and tallies the number of degrees conferred in each. For this look into the impact of college on how students are taught to think, I have grouped the fields of study into three broad categories. The percentage of graduates in each of the three is shown in the following table.

Liberal Arts and Education	46%
Professional	40%
Technical	14%

Liberal Arts and Education is dominated by social sciences and history (10% of all college graduates), psychology (6%), education (6%), the arts (5%), communications (5%), and traditional liberal arts programs such as English, humanities and philosophy. These fields examine human behavior, interpersonal relations and societal dynamics. They differ from studies in the professional and technical categories in a fundamental way. They explore treatises, sociological postulates and behavioral theories. The students are taught to be comparative thinkers, to compare and contrast, but never to reach a rigid conclusion; rather, to consider, and equally weight, all possibilities, all ideas and all theories.

Professional degrees include business, computer science, health care, law enforcement and agriculture. In these fields, students study the methods needed to provide services or to operate an enterprise. The courses concentrate on various aspects of the field, exploring the challenges they will face and identifying the tools and methods that have been proven in the past to be effective at working through issues and problems. Students in these fields are encouraged to think methodically.

Technical fields include Biology, Medicine, Physics, Chemistry, Mathematics and Engineering. The foundation of these is critical thinking. To try to master real things in a real world, and apply that knowledge to physical reality, students are expected to critically examine the subject at hand, to arrive at conclusions that can be proven or to construct things that will work and last.

Walk into a park. Watch the birds, feel the grass, smell the air. What does it tell you? Common sense tells you that it's wonderful and to be enjoyed. Critical thinking provokes interest in where it came from, what it's made of, and how it all works. Methodical thinking causes you to dissect its pieces and find ways to maintain or improve it. Comparative thinking tells you it's something to be parsed, contrasted with other ecosystems, and compared with other worlds that theoretically exist. In their separate worlds, critical thinkers accept reality, methodical thinkers try to improve it, and comparative thinkers assign value to it.

There are two vectors that send these thinkers on different paths. The direction of one is toward realism. Ninety degrees from it, the other direction is toward surrealism, meaning in a direction that leads toward a result or conclusion that is essentially unverifiable. In other words, towards what is hoped for, imagined or perceived, and is potentially unreal.

Students in technical fields are schooled to think along the path of realism. If an idea cannot be physically proven, it is not accepted. If a structure won't withstand hurricanes or earthquakes, it can't be built. If cells don't respond to new drugs favorably, they aren't prescribed.

Comparative thinkers tend in the direction of surrealism. For some fields, like sociology, it is a mountain range of theories, different peaks with unique views, but offering only observations, not answers. In the social sciences, piles of surveys and tables of demographic statistics provide interesting insights, but in the end, no real conclusions. Humanities and history are stacks of stories and reams of themes, yet though they offer possible explanations, none are provably real.

Methodical thinking trends generally on the realism path but often takes an angle toward surrealism. Legal studies examine cartloads of case law, and seemingly come to a conclusion, until the underlying law itself is revised, or until an unexpected new case changes things. Law enforcement studies consider proven methods for dealing with individuals and specific situations, but veer toward the surreal when exploring overall law enforcement strategies or crime prevention programs.

In our daily lives, as we react to events or respond to situations, the two vectors have more concrete applications. In one direction, there is what is known; in the other, what is not known. A lone woman is on the side of a rural two-lane road with a flat tire, miles from town, and is unable to loosen the lug nuts. A man pulls over and offers his help. She is in a situation where there are some things that she knows based on the man's appearance and demeanor, but there are many more things she doesn't know. In the end, she relies on common sense to accept the man's offer or to send him away.

In the modern world, saturated with advertising and marketing streaming from unending media, we are constantly making decisions or passing judgment on what is being shown or told. We filter the claims and sales pitches through thinking. People who have not completed a college field of study primarily rely on their common sense and the critical thinking skills they have developed. College graduates instead filter the information with the kind of thinking learned in their field of study. This difference is trivial when deciding on most things, such as buying the latest gadget, selecting a used car, or accepting an offer to help with a flat tire. But in some arenas, different thinking processes can result in profoundly different cognitive results.

The role of diet on human health has been one such topic for decades. Claims cover specific foods, food groups, food sources, vitamin supplements, herbs, food processing, preservatives, genetic modification, and the list goes on. There have been countless assertions with a host of unknowns. We could just ignore each assertion; a good many people do. On the other hand, some think about it. A simple example is butter. It was claimed to be bad for you. A common sense approach might lead to an outright rejection of the claim, or a hedge to cut back on consumption. Critical thinking examines all elements of the claim, including the language used to support it. It considers the consumption levels warned against. It examines chemical-biological research behind it. Then it evaluates the claimed risk versus known benefits. Methodical thinking doesn't directly question the validity of the claim. It also evaluates the risk versus benefit, but from a process and methods, or business approach, rather than from a technical perspective. Comparative thinking also doesn't directly question the validity of the claim, as the assumption is that any theory deserves proper consideration. Rather than a risk versus benefit review, the thinking hinges on a believable versus not-credible evaluation, comparing this claim, and its proponents, with similar claims. These three college-taught ways of thinking lead the graduates to make a decision about butter along different thought vectors.

In the realm of public policy, and the ideological bases undergirding it, the ways of thinking can lead to diverging paths. Public policy uses the authority and power of government to achieve beneficial outcomes, theoretically. At some levels, it is straight forward. An interstate highway system, funded by all, benefits all. At other levels, it is more intangible. Reducing air pollution is an example. Here, it is a meld of cost versus benefit, questionable claims and studies, and contingent on definitions of good and better. It is an attempt to tackle an exceptionally complex set of issues with written regulations. Assertions are made, research is explained, and predictions are suggested. Ultimately, a proposed course of action, a policy, is dumped into the political machinery for adjudication. The voters, or their representatives, face a decision. The thinking begins.

The purpose of a policy is to achieve certain outcomes. It does so by generating outputs. Comparative thinking focuses on the predicted outcomes, contrasting the status quo with the expected status quo ante. If alternative policy approaches are offered, their different outcomes, not their mechanisms, are examined. Any cost versus benefit analysis is confined to total projected program cost against the frequently fiscally unquantifiable benefit. So it becomes a normative evaluation. Methodical thinking looks at both the outcomes and the outputs, but as a business calculation, not in terms of technical feasibility. With both ways of thinking, the proposed end point of the policy dominates the thought process. In contrast, the critical thinker focuses on the policy's outputs, and then does an analysis of the potential effectiveness of the outputs, including their unintended manifestations, to arrive at an assessment of how the outputs could achieve the intended outcomes. The common sense thinker takes a similar approach, because that is what daily real life teaches, what experience reminds us and practical knowledge encourages.

The table shown earlier reveals that 40% of graduates earn Liberal Arts and Education degrees. Over seven hundred thousand people with these degrees take their place in society each year, and along with them, a way of thinking that is different. Although comparative thinkers comprise a small minority of the population, they exert an outsized influence on society at large. A good many become lawyers, journalists, social workers, staff members or teachers. They populate the institutions that the general population looks to for information, understanding and expertise, including media outlets, government social and human services agencies, universities and advocacy groups. They also fill the public schools as teachers and administrators where their thinking sets the tone for writing the curricula and presenting the subject matter.

Different ways of thinking is an important social dynamic. Dr. John Gray described how men and women think differently in his famous 1992 book, *Men Are From Mars and Women Are From Venus*[5]. He made the point that men and women must understand each other's thinking in order to treat one another well and maintain positive relationships. He described how their way of thinking propels men and women to act, react and make decisions differently. He explained how hurtful arguments can be tempered or avoided, and emotional issues resolved, when men and women recognize the thinking that compels them. Understanding this is what made Dr. Gray's book not only popular, but effective at getting different kinds of thinkers to better understand one another. It made people realize that in a given situation, male and female thinking can lead men and women to different conclusions, sparking different reactions.

In a similar way, critical, methodical or comparative thinking can lead people when faced with the same circumstances or in view of the same facts to reach alternative, sometimes even contradictory conclusions. Thinking can cause people to react differently to change, to events or to new proposals.

The next few chapters examine relatively small segments of the population that exert tremendous influence on American society: school teachers, college professors and those in the media. Most of them are comparative thinkers.

The American School

Education used to be the objective in public schools. Now, students are being schooled. Rather than being taught how to think, students are being taught what to think.

This shift has been the subject of books and essays for several decades, if not half a century. I won't summarize the theories or rehash the analyses. Like so much of our world, change is the result of a near infinite interplay of factors, great complexity, and the uncertainties of turbulence and chaos. Changes in society, as in this evolution in education, share this description of change in general. Research into it may have generated all sorts of explanations as to the effects and their causes, but in the final analysis, there is no comprehensive answer. It simply involves too many people, too many factors and too much serendipity.

So, I'll simply assert that the change has taken place and avoid the why. Instead, consider the thinking of those who run the schools, and how they have come to believe that American communities must accept, or at least submit to this change.

Education is highly valued in America. Parents, grandparents, even adults without children appreciate the need for everyone to receive a good education. An educated electorate is vital to the health of a republican form of government. Voters must have a foundation of civic knowledge and the ability to exercise sound thinking in order to sift through the noise of political campaigns.

Yet despite broad support for an education system that was delivering quality, school teachers and administrators were able to implement wholesale change. This might seem an impossible campaign to execute in a country with a population of over three hundred million. Actually, it's not that difficult. Consider the table below that shows the number of teachers in the United States[6].

	Total Number	Percent of U.S. Population
K-6 Teachers	1,908K	0.57%
7-12 Teachers	1,920K	0.58%

Although there are many teachers, they are a quite small percentage of the population. Teachers share much in common. They are all college educated. They work in an environment that is physically isolated from the rest of society. They follow a fixed daily routine and a regular calendar with no surprises other than an occasional snow day. For the most part, they don't interact with other adults. Most, literally, control the population that they do interact with, their students. Other than periodic administrative performance evaluations and subjective classroom monitoring, they face few expectations, have minimal supervision and receive little feedback on their effectiveness. In a sense, they inhabit an environment that is separated from the reality that the rest of the population faces every day.

Many teachers have a limited knowledge of the enterprises that employ most Americans. They have not been exposed to the kind of organizational dynamics, physical processes or material realities that most enterprises deal with. Most elementary teachers majored in education or psychology and know little else. Some secondary teachers majored in the sciences or mathematics that they teach, but a good many graduate with an education degree that may or may not have included a minor in the subject they end up teaching.

From the early years when teaching became an organized profession, it was devoted to improving how to teach. New instructional methods were improvised, better text books were written and organizational changes introduced. Teacher education became more standardized and incorporated advances in child psychology. Tests and testing were improved.

In more recent decades, as mentioned earlier, teachers have played a proactive role in determining what should be taught. This is not an entirely new development. As early as the 1840's, Horace Mann called for reforms to public education. Following the Civil War, education for freed slaves who had limited experience as citizen participants prompted the need to include civics in the curriculum. Assimilation and character development were topical following the immigrant wave at the beginning of the twentieth century, and carried into the reform movement of John Dewey in the 1920's. But this work gained a new momentum beginning in the 1960's when counter-culture movements and post-modern philosophies and reasoning took root. By 1980, the first volume of a journal dedicated to this was published: "Discourse: Studies in the Cultural Politics of Education."

Among elementary and secondary school educators, a quite small number control the curricula and determine what is to be taught, and how. They write and approve the text books. They suggest the reading lists. They decide which tests to use to evaluate student knowledge, to assess teacher performance and to evaluate the effectiveness of the educational system in general.

	Total Number	Percent of U.S. Population
Principals	116K	0.03%
Superintendents	14K	0.004%

The table reveals that the number of people who set the agenda for elementary and secondary education across the country is by any measure a small group. They are tightly knit professionals who attend the same conferences, read the same journals and come from the rather insular world of teachers. How they think, and what they think drives what the population under age 18 is taught to believe. They influence the minds of a sizeable segment of the population, those aged 6 to 18, about 54 million.

If the premise asserted at the start of this essay, that education is now more focused on teaching students what to think, it is appropriate to examine what principals and superintendents think and believe, and most teachers as well. Being products of a college education, which is dominated by the progressive world view in terms of the culture, societal norms and principles for democratic government, it follows naturally that teachers adopt these views.

In the past, those in positions of influence and authority took pains to separate their opinions and policy wishes from their professional duties and the strictures of their institution. It used to be this way with teachers, principals and superintendents. Yet, over the last several decades, they supplanted their professional responsibilities with becoming advocates for their opinions and beliefs. They didn't do it from outside pressure. They did it because they were convinced that it was the right thing to do. It may sound strange, but they also did it because 'everyone else' was doing the same thing. In this case, the 'everyone else' was their fellow school superintendents and principals, sharing articles in education journals and later, notes on educator web sites, and spreading ideas at seminars and conferences. Advancing cultural progress had become the proper, perhaps even the moral thing to do.

Educators' immersion in progressive world views may have provided the motivation to initiate change, but that alone was insufficient to enact it. Institutions, including education, are inherently resistant to change. Because the status quo is generally meeting obligations and achieving a reasonable level of success, institutional leadership and the broader community are reluctant to disrupt the system. Change is introduced incrementally and tentatively implemented after serious deliberation.

The usual reaction to change is: if it isn't broken, don't fix it. Actually, that is the common sense one. When presented with a new alternative for the status quo, comparative thinking simply contrasts what is with what could be. It doesn't much evaluate why the status quo exists or how it was reached. Almost any new idea that offers a potentially improved outcome is reason enough to jettison the present for a possible future.

Teachers compassionately press for better schooling with the best of intentions. The world view they acquired in college and reinforced within their professional associations inspires them to step away from the past, as reflected in the status quo, and to make progress by moving forward. Their mode of thinking, also reinforced by those around them, causes them to contrast new concepts primarily against the improved future outcomes they suggest.

Put another way, among a group that believes most everything is broken, everything needs to be fixed. Lacking an education on provable facts and the uncertainties that reside in complex systems, and inhabiting a community insulated from many of the realities that others contend with, they are more open to new explanations and less critical of the details. They think about things, but tend to limit their thinking when their feelings and opinions are confirmed.

This is, of course, a host of generalizations about a segment of the population, teachers and educators. The generalizations become more acute as we look at two other slices of the population.

The American Campus

Universities are highly respected in the United States. They are not quite revered, as in France, nor honored, as in the United Kingdom, nor worshipped for its intellectual superiority, as in Germany. They are, rather, highly esteemed for spreading knowledge, advancing science and contributing to the general welfare. With this reputation, the University is positioned to exert tremendous influence on the country.

Considering the relatively small population of professors and college administrators, it is not a stretch to describe this great influence as outsized. It takes two paths in affecting the general public. Directly, it educates Americans, in growing numbers. Indirectly, through published papers, public appearances, participation in conferences and commissions, it generates popular news, informs advocacy groups and affects public policy.

As with K-12 education over the last several decades, there has been significant change on the university campus. Like K-12 education, there have been many studies commissioned and research papers published analyzing the change and passing judgment on it. A review of this work and a critique of their themes is not the point. However, there are elements of the change that are relevant to this examination into the outsize influence of the university. First, there has been a great increase both in the number and size of institutions and in the number of students. Roughly 0.4 million students graduated from college in 1960. In 1979 it was almost 0.8 million, over one million in 1990, and 1.8 million in 2015[7].

Second, there has been an expansion in degree programs. In an earlier essay, degree programs were grouped in three categories: Professional, Liberal Arts and Education, and Technical. Remarkably, since 1970, the percentage in each category has remained relatively constant. But in the second category, there have been some significant changes. Education degrees dropped from 22% to 6%. Communications and journalism grew from around 1% to almost 5%. New and expanding area studies, humanities and other interdisciplinary degrees grew as well. Although it is somewhat of a generalization, the trend in the Liberal Arts and Education fields of study has more students pursuing degrees in fields that are more subjective.

Third, it is widely acknowledged that the university faculty is dominated by people who share similar opinions on many issues. The effect of this on higher education has been the subject of various books and essays. Some of the concerns raised include the vitality of the curricula, the impact on fostering new or dissenting viewpoints, the role of education in promoting civil discourse, the ability of the institution to advance science and knowledge, and even the value of a college education in general. Although many scholars argue persuasively that this has significantly impacted American culture and politics, for this discussion, the focus is on how the thinking of a like-minded university faculty exerts its influence on the American Story.

In the first essay on individual Americans, I presented a little county of 155 employed people to represent the 155 million full time employees active in the United States. Fourteen people were employed in education. Of the fourteen, there is only a fifty-fifty chance that one of them is a college professor. Looking at the nation-wide numbers, we see that they comprise hardly a fraction of the workforce. Of the roughly 500,000 professors in the country, they are further broken down in thirds: professors, associate professors and assistant professors. The titles are meaningful to them, but not so much to those beyond the campus. Yet, they are an indicator of the degree of influence that they exert. The upper layers, the professors and the associate professors at a combined strength of about 340,000, generally set the agenda and the tone.

For the moment, let's reconsider the total number of professors, about 500,000. I'll apportion this number into the field of study categories highlighted earlier and see how many professors there are that have been educated to adopt different methods of thinking. It is broken down in the table below.

Method of Thinking	Percent	Number of Professors
Critical	14%	70,000
Methodical	40%	200,000
Comparative	46%	230,000

The comparative thinking segment of the university is particularly influential. Directly, they educate the very small number of newspaper publishers, TV and movie producers and a relatively small number of K-12 administrators. They also educate almost all of the members of the workforces of the various media outlets: the print journalists, the television reporters, the crews who produce the TV shows and the movies. They educate almost all of the teachers. Their way of thinking is instilled in the relatively small number of the population who craft the American Story and who run the American School.

Taking together the professors, the print publishers, and the media moguls, some call them the 'elite.' I believe it is an unhelpful label. They don't see themselves as a separate class of human beings. They have spent their lives in studies and research to learn who people are, what they do, and how they are motivated. They believe that they have their thumb on the pulse of human nature, that they understand and can explain the human condition. They feel that they can give reality its human expression. They are providing an essential service by condensing their knowledge and wisdom in terms that average people can understand; then they pass it along in news analysis, television reporting, documentaries, dramatic films and even comedic depictions.

But as bright and learned as the professors and their powerful former students are, they remain a product of their environment. It is like a veneer on an otherwise rich, complex and diversified American society. They are cloistered on a campus, be it an academic or media one, surrounded by like-minded individuals, unconnected to any kind of customer, receiving regular paychecks whatever the weather, the events or the vagaries of the marketplace. They are real people, but they live in a surreal, perhaps even unreal environment. Yet they are the experts, the explainers, the ones who can describe what human nature implants in our curious minds: cause and effect.

And the cause is almost always binary. It is comparative. It is this (this being simplified and condensed), or that (similarly distilled). Along the way, there may be introduced an alternative, which is substituted for either this or that, or which modifies one or the other. But there remains the binary choice.

In a way, it goes back to those who can understand and accept that there is complexity, chaos, uncertainty and unpredictability, and those who can't. Contrast most professors with a different very small corner of the population, the chemists, the biologists and the nuclear physicists. I am speaking here of the advanced research chemists, the molecular and sub-molecular biologists, and experimental nuclear physicists. Their studies delve into the world of the phenomenal. If you should ever have the opportunity to meet some of these practitioners, I suggest that you take the time to get to know them and have them explain what they know. It will take some effort, because they have learned that their field of knowledge and understanding is essentially alien to the average person. They tend to smile a lot. They have insights well beyond the binary, cause and effect thinking that passes for conventional, societal thinking. They live in a world of mystery, inexplicability and acceptance of things that just happen to be the way they are. Most of their body of knowledge has been discovered by accident. Some discoveries point to new directions, to different experiments, to alternative materials. On rare occasions, a collection of experimental results may seem to gel so as to introduce some kind of theory. Equally rarely, a thought experiment extrapolated from prior discovered knowledge may lead to a general theory. Even in these cases, knowledge, or truth, if you will, is reached by accurately describing the effects of interactions, the resulting output of mixtures, or the products of previously unexplored phenomena. Any theory may be interesting, but it is essentially irrelevant until it can be verified by rigorous experimentation.

These narrow fields of science concentrate almost exclusively on effects. The causes are rarely important. Most of the time, they will tell you, the cause is unknowable. At best, the cause is merely a guess. Consider nuclear fission of uranium. Nuclear physicists gained a sound enough understanding of it to give engineers the tools to fabricate and operate uranium-fueled nuclear reactors in the 1950's. If an atom of uranium-235 absorbs a neutron, it will most likely cause the uranium atom to split, to fission. The conditions and materials to promote controllable fission are well known. There are models for describing how this may happen, but the precise cause remains unknown. When the uranium atom splits, it creates two new atoms which are called fission products. How many of which fission products are created has been precisely determined. But the reason for this distribution of fission products, the cause for it, is simply a guess.

The contrast between the thinking and the approach of those in the fields of science mentioned above is in sharp contrast to that of the comparative thinking that drives the social sciences. The former views nature as comprised of multivariate, complex, phenomena-filled chaotic systems. The latter sees the world as a decipherable system wherein two or more driving factors, or causes, generate certain results, or effects. The former accepts, dare I say, the reality that within systems, causes are unknowable, whereas the latter is devoted to attributing effects to causes.

The American Story

The American Story herein refers to the day by day depiction of America that is portrayed in the media. It is told in newspapers and magazines, and in televised newscasts and documentaries. Further, it is reflected and reinforced in television shows, plays and movies.

Those who produce and distribute the stories, which become The Story that fill our days, wield tremendous influence on public opinion. Their number is remarkably small, as the following table reveals[8].

	Total Number	Percent of U.S. Population
Newspaper	183,200	0.06%
Periodicals	93,600	0.03%
Movie Production	239,000	0.07%
TV Production	130,000	0.04%
Total	645,800	0.2%

These numbers are the total employment in each area. Only a fraction of the totals are the people who decide which stories to tell, who write them and who edit them. These senior writers, producers and editors comprise a stunningly small number of individuals.

There are about 1,300 newspapers in the country. Each has one editor in chief, meaning 1,300 people guide what becomes the printed news every day. They and a handful of associate editors direct what events the reporters will cover, what words or phrases to apply, and approve the final version of each article. They also choose which wire service stories and which syndicated columns to run. They cull the letters they receive and decide which to print. And, of course, they write the editorials. The exact number of editors, associate editors and senior writers is not important. Even if it was ten at each newspaper, or 13,000 nationwide, it's quite a small number when contrasted with the entire population.

The description of the press room also applies to the roughly 1,700 television stations in the country. Only a handful of executive producers and owners decide what to air and what news to report.

Local papers and small market television stations rely heavily on the news wires and national networks for national and international news. The Associated Press is the dominant player, whose web site says it employs 3,200. At its New York headquarters, a fraction of this number sets the guidelines and decides which articles to distribute. Again, it is a relatively small cadre of people who are in control.

There are around 7,200 magazines published in the United States. Of course, they cover a wide range of topics beyond the news. Many are devoted to popular culture, such as People and Better Homes and Gardens. Still, they reach a wide audience and have great influence on trends, fads and opinions. And they too are controlled by small staffs of senior editors.

Movies and television shows don't craft The Story. However, they play a major role in reflecting it on film, thereby reinforcing its messages and promoting its prevalence. We'll look at this aspect later on, after exploring the nature of the daily and weekly news.

What is news and what is newsworthy? It would seem that the answer to these two questions is straightforward. News, of course, is events. The news that is newsworthy would then seem to be those events of interest or importance to the general public. Even in this simplistic description, we see that what becomes the news can be quite subjective. Someone must decide what is interesting or important.

Someone must also decide what constitutes an event. Weather is always a big part of the news, although it isn't really news because we can see what the weather is simply by looking outside the window. It is weather forecasts that are newsworthy. A traffic accident fatality may be news, because most likely it tied up the highway for hours and inconvenienced thousands of people. A fender-bender that simply slowed traffic for some moments isn't news: it happens all the time. Unless, of course, it leads to a drug bust or an arrest of a politician for driving under the influence. An angry father contesting a new town ordnance doesn't make the news; unless, of course, his ire includes beating someone in the audience. And if he waves a gun around the town hall, well, that will make the local news, maybe even find its way on the national airwaves. A volcano erupting in Hawaii: great graphics and great news. The oozing lava that has flowed from it for several decades, day after day: hardly news. A person dies at hospice – not news. A person alleged to have been mistreated by the staff who subsequently died: news on an otherwise slow news day. Three Senegalese misfits kill thirty school children with machetes for whatever reason: the proverbial tree falling in a forest where no one is there to hear it. Oprah admitting that she has a tattoo of Johnny Depp but won't say where: news for two weeks! A murder in Sicily; not news. A murder in Sicily by a descendant of Michael Corleone's godmother: now that's a story (and thus, news). But at least these examples are news based on actual events.

The Story includes non-events that are deemed newsworthy. The results of polls and surveys are one such kind of non-event. Polls are not spontaneous or random, as are most news events. They are planned and conducted by organizations. Volumes have been written about polls and polling, particularly in the context of political campaigns and elections[9]. Pollsters, marketers and politicians want a sense of how much confidence to place in polls. Questions abound: are they accurate; do they represent the broader public; can they be manipulated; do they reflect opinions, attitudes or both; are respondents honest in their answers; on and on. These are important questions, but they are not pertinent to the role of polls in creating a national narrative. The salient point is that polls are reported as stories that analyze and interpret the results. They provide the opportunity to present the interpretation, that is, the opinion of the news organization, as factual news.

Press releases can become newsworthy. Newsrooms and individual reporters receive scores of press releases each week. Some announce true events, as when a local business is awarded a big contract, when an organization hires a new executive, or when someone is given a prestigious award. Others come from special interest or advocacy organizations. Their releases can announce actual events. But they often present non-events. The release may be a way to disseminate a particular policy approach, to advance an agenda, or to sway public opinion. Examples include an environmental group's report card on the health of lakes or bays, a human rights group's list of racist organizations and a policy advocate group's announcement of a new research study that describes this or that. Publishers and producers decide which are newsworthy or not. They further decide how the information in the release will be written up or aired. This becomes another way that news organizations can influence The Story that reaches the eyes and ears of Americans nationwide.

Another kind of non-event is the academic paper. It wends its way into one of a myriad of journals; the field where publish or perish resides. Frequently grounded in the thesis of some doctoral student, the research can challenge an established theory by publishing new research that calls it into question. Recently in vogue, some reports focus on new research in behavioral economics. Others take a new twist on sociology, anthropology or psychology. In the last several decades, papers have described new theories of possible causal relationships found in group studies. As with polls and press releases, they are summarized and condensed into a column in the newspaper or a short segment on the nightly news broadcast. The footnotes are left behind; the references are ignored; the validity of the data is unexplored; countervailing theories and research are rarely mentioned. Most importantly, they are written as though the insights are all fresh and new, unique to history, as if the same or similar conclusions have never before been reached by previous scholars. If the editors and producers like the abstract of a research paper, it becomes news[10]. Because it comes from an academic expert, its assertions are portrayed as facts, and its conclusions painted as a kind of truth.

Finally, there is factual news. It includes stock market listings, game scores and league standings, and weather related numbers, such as yesterdays high and low temperatures and snowfall amounts. It is daily data; we take it for granted. Yet even in this news category, someone decides what is newsworthy – what daily data to report and what to omit.

The news disseminated daily and weekly is presumed to be a complete and factual depiction of current events and ground truth. In fact, it may be so only coincidentally. More often than not, it is a collection of stories that portray a sense of reality. It may be printed with real words and broadcast as real images on the television screen. But it may actually be unreal or surreal. It could simply be an illusion.

Someone decides what will be printed or broadcast. What influences their thinking, and what animates their judgment is critical to their decision-making.

Producers, editors and writers have much in common. Most are college graduates with degrees in the arts, English, communications and journalism. Their careers frequently demand long hours, making them spend most of their time working and living inside what is a tightly-knit community, a cloistered one if you will, surrounded by their peers. In a sense, they don't face the economic and commercial realities that drive the enterprises that employ most Americans. They have essentially no personal interaction with their customers (they view them through the lens of demographic groups), and there is no opportunity for them to receive substantive feedback from them. Their income is divorced from the product they deliver, in that it is derived from circulation, market share or the box office take. The moment they finish the day's stories, it is on to a clean sheet of paper the next day. They inhabit a surreal environment doing unique work. They are sequestered, if not isolated, from their readers and their audience.

Within the major news organizations, most truly and honestly believe that they are highly enlightened, broadly educated and altruistically intentioned. Bolstered by this, and because they associate almost exclusively with one another, they believe that their worldview is, in fact, the main stream. Their Story fills the popular publications and television screens across the country. It is also, very importantly, the only news that penetrates their own press room or television studio. The very stories and programs that they themselves produce become their view of reality, their understanding of the outside world.

	Number of Executives
1,300 Newspapers	5,000
200 News Periodicals	1,000
1,700 TV News Stations	6,000
Total	12,000

The news that is written and the news programs that are produced come from a very small number of outlets, revisited in the table above. The table also lists the approximate number of executives who control the content: the senior editors, publishers and producers.

Let's go back to the coliseum. If you're sitting in the stands, across the field sit all the movers and shakers that dominate what you read and watch every day – the roughly 12,000 people listed above. They fill just over one-tenth of the stadium. They are all hanging out with one another; they are all having similar conversations. They know you are out there, filling the other seats. Other than the fact that you might have bought a ticket, they see you as merely the crowd. They think they know you, your life and your country.

There's no conspiracy to misrepresent America. It happens quite naturally. Media people are obviously active thinkers, articulate speakers and compelling writers. But most are members of one tribe, intellectually, who share a set of beliefs and have a common way of thinking that is different than many other Americans. The Story comes from a mere handful of people, and they look at things, experience things, and think about things differently than just about everyone else. Yet they own the Story.

Thus far, the focus has been on the news media's role in creating and disseminating the Story. But, of course, that is not the whole story, if you will. The entertainment media has a far broader reach than the news media. The earlier table listed total employment in the fields of media: newspapers, periodicals, movies and television. Except perhaps in the newspaper field, the other fields are dominated by people who produce entertainment. This is almost exclusively the case in movies, and mostly the case in television. Most periodicals are devoted to some form of entertainment. Consider the array of magazines in the racks at the supermarket checkout. Scan the titles in the magazine section at the bookstore. Among the top fifty magazines by circulation, only one, "Time," is (primarily) devoted to news and events, with a circulation well below that of "Good Housekeeping" and "Game Informer." The entertainment in magazines pretty much focuses on popular culture: food, health, beauty and fashion, hobbies, celebrities, etc. They don't tell much in the way of stories, but they highlight trends and help promote fads.

Movies and television shows are exceptionally influential in painting the American human landscape. They are the purest and most powerful form of storytelling: vivid videos, crisp dialogue and stirring music. They are also very expensive to produce. It is no wonder that their production is controlled by an astonishingly small number of major studios (movies) or networks (TV). Your coliseum, the nine surrounding it, the other 330 sets of ten beyond them, filled with people like you and your neighbors, are subjected to the production choices of barely two dozen meeting rooms, each dominated by a few peerless persons.

Returning again to our coliseum, these few senior producers occupy the color commentator seats in the press box. Their descriptions and analysis fill the television sets in millions of homes and sports bars. Their comments go to the meaning behind the play by play, to the reasons for how the game is being played, to the nuance and subtle interpersonal relations that influence The Story.

Like the news producers, editors and writers, movie and TV show producers also come from the same or similar mold. But their community is far more insular and much more cloistered from the individuals who comprise the box office numbers. And, in a very real way, they live in world of fiction, of make-believe, because that is what they produce. They fashion stories that viewers watch through the lens of the willing suspension of disbelief. Yet the messages that they deliver are absorbed and believed.

Even more so than news producers, film producers believe they are uniquely positioned not only by being able to portray what average people do, but also because they can describe people's hearts and souls. Being artistically equipped to illustrate right versus wrong, good versus evil and just versus unjust, they define the morality behind The Story.

The American Portrayal is a product of our schools, colleges and media. On a daily and weekly basis it may influence public opinion. It may even influence elected officials to write new laws or take specific governmental action. But in the months preceding an election, it can play a powerful role in affecting how people vote. Political operatives know this. The next two chapters explore this by examining the political parties and the voters.

American Parties

Although a divided America is an illusion, the divide between Democrats and Republicans is real and it is stark, particularly at the national level. Coming later is a side by side look at the 2016 party platforms. The Table of Contents is reprinted and the main points of the preambles are listed.

The two documents are remarkably different in terms of approach and subject matter, let alone the positions taken on various issues. The Republican approach is based on the principles that guide the platform, particularly governing principles. The Democratic platform, despite references to values and rights, takes a policy approach. The Democratic platform covers a broad range of subject matter, a plethora of policy objectives in numerous areas, including race relations, voting and climate change. In contrast, the Republican platform focuses on topics, primarily economic growth, de-regulation, limiting the power and reach of the federal government, immigration control and energy policy.

Issue by issue there is little commonality. The Republican platform stresses equality of opportunity while the Democratic one stresses the means to achieve equality of outcomes. The Republican approach strives to comply with the Constitution while the Democratic one stresses greater democracy and emphasizes a kind of majority rule that the Constitution sought to constrain. The Democratic platform sees America's leadership role as one based on encouraging common global action by developing and negotiating with partners while the Republican platform sees a role in which an economically and militarily strong United States inspires cooperation and deters aggressors.

In areas where they agree there is need for improvement or change, the prescriptions take different directions. In criminal justice reform, education, and financial regulation, there are differences of opinion, and these areas may in fact be the few in which the parties seem to have common ground for effective policy-making. In healthcare, however, the two parties are poles apart, even though both support Medicare and Medicaid.

The Democratic platform wades into some areas that the Republican platform does not address at all. These include gender pay equality, man-made climate change, free college education, systemic racism and wealth inequality. There is a commitment at the national level to protect what the Democratic platform identifies as its values, most associated with demographic groups, international health and human rights issues, and others.

Finally, although both platforms decry the other party's performance, the Democratic platform goes a step further. Its platform states that congressional Republicans have chosen dysfunction over trying to find solutions, and describes the Republican nominee as someone who appeals to base differences rather than a better nature, and assigns these sentiments to Republicans in general. In other words, its platform makes the point that the opposing party is motivated by something other than caring or compassion.

The following columns summarize the 2016 Republican and Democratic Party platforms. The first two are the text of the table of contents. The second two summarize each preamble.

Republican Table of Contents

1. Restoring the American Dream.
2. A Rebirth of Constitutional Government.
3. Americas Natural Resources: Agriculture, Energy, and the Environment.
4. Government Reform.
5. Great American Families, Education, Healthcare and Criminal Justice.
6. America Resurgent.

Democratic Table of Contents

1. Raise Incomes and Restore Economic Security for the Middle Class.
2. Create Good-Paying Jobs.
3. Fight for Economic Fairness and Against Inequality.
4. Bring Americans Together and Remove Barriers to Opportunities.
5. Protect Voting Rights, Fix Our Campaign Finance System, and Restore Our Democracy.
6. Combat Climate Change, Build a Clean Energy Economy, and Secure Environmental Justice.
7. Provide Quality and Affordable Education.
8. Ensure the Health and Safety of All Americans.
9. Principled Leadership.
10. Support Our Troops and Keep Faith with Our Veterans.
11. Confront Global Threats.
12. Protect Our Values.
13. A Leader in the World.

Republican Platform Preamble: Reaffirm the principles that unite us.

1. Constitution is a covenant.
   - for political and economic freedom.
2. Peace through strength.
3. Wrong direction past eight years.
   - stagnant growth and wages.
   - international weakness.

- imposed costly health care system that doesn't work and limits freedom.
  - doubled the debt.
  - borders left open.
  - waged war on energy.
  - over-regulating.
4. Reduce bureaucrat power and de-regulate.
5. Return control to people and the states.

Democratic Platform Preamble: Belief that out of many, we are one.

1. America is great but not perfect. We can make it better.
2. Great progress last eight years.
3. Too many Americans left out and behind.
  - stagnant wages.
  - income inequality
  - Republican gridlock prevents solutions.
4. We are stronger together.
  - sustainable growth.
  - more economic fairness.
  - common vs. self-interest.
  - long term investments (not short ones).
5. Gross wealth inequality; 20 richest = bottom 150 million.
6. American racism persists and must be faced.
7. Cradle to college education.
8. Equal pay for women.
9. Maintain Social Security.
10. End Wall Street greed and illegal acts.
11. Repeal Citizen's United.
12. Maintain voting rights.
13. Climate change is a real and urgent threat; become the clean energy superpower.
14. Lead the world with principle and purpose; mobilize common global action.
15. Diversity is our promise.
16. Proud heritage as a nation of immigrants.
17. Protect civil rights and liberties.
18. Republican nominee appeals to basest differences.

19. We can make it better: more just economy, more equal society, more perfect union.

The Democratic platform document was 55 pages long, set in the kind of dense type typically found in academic papers. The Republican document was 61 pages long, not quite as dense, and formatted more as a business plan than a research paper. Thoroughly reading the two would reveal how very different they are from one another. But the two sets of columns tersely highlight these differences. The two parties differ not only on the substance of issues and governing approach. They have, for lack of a better term, cultural differences. They write differently, they seem to have their own vernacular and they perceive the makeup, motivations and interests of the target audience from different vantage points. This may be because, as some have suggested, that party platforms are targeted at the party base, not at the electorate in general. That may be true. But the base is the ground team for the campaign. The party platform is their guide, the summation that becomes their talking points and the ammunition for their arguments. It is the narrative for the messages that find their way into campaign advertisements and for the speeches that are given at rallies. They put flesh on the ideological bones of the party.

An earlier chapter discussed American values; how they are fairly definable and generally accepted. The set of three columns that comes next lists these American values and compares them to the policy and position statements in the party platforms.

American Value	Democratic Platform	Republican Platform
Legacy Government	Majority Rule	Constitutional Rule
Civil/Criminal Justice	Disparate Impact	Rule of Law

Equal Opportunity	Equal Outcomes	Accepted
Personal Control	Government Guidelines	Accepted
Free Enterprise	Wealth Distribution	Accepted
Practicality	(not mentioned)	(not mentioned)
Directness / Honesty	(not mentioned)	Accepted
Free K-12 Education	Accepted	Accepted
Modern		
Regulate Monopolies	Regulate More Broadly	Accepted
Anti-Trust	Accepted	Accepted
Regulate Money Markets	Accepted	Accepted
Progressive Taxes	Accepted	Accepted
Social Security	Accepted	Accepted
Medicare / Medicaid	Accepted	Accepted
Unemployment Insurance	Accepted	Accepted
Clean Environment	Global Warming	Accepted
Assimilating Immigrants	Open Borders	Controlled
Unique		
Community Standards	Government Guidelines	Accepted
Charities	Accepted	Accepted
Civic Organizations	Government Guidelines	Accepted
Informality	(not mentioned)	(not mentioned)
Mutual Respect	Government Guidelines	Accepted
Accepting Change	Government Guidelines	Accepted

You may disagree with the way the comparison has been constructed and the shorthand used to label how the party platforms compare with American values. And obviously, simplifying the comparisons to columns in a few words avoids the full discussion of the details that would provide better understanding. Yet, the columns illustrate an important point. The Republican platform more closely aligns with American values. The Democratic platform does in some areas, but in others it ignores them, and in a few instances it replaces them.

The Democratic Party Platform of 2016 does not articulate the governing principles that underpin it. The inspiring rhetorical references to unique aspects of American character and American values of earlier platforms are gone. It is filled with policy prescriptions, but the source of their philosophical or ideological foundation is not expressed. An honest reading concludes that much of it is inspired by socialist ideology. As such, it is a document that at its core is not consistent with American values.

The American Voter

The goal in American elections is as simple as it can be: get more votes than any other candidate. With the Electoral College, Presidential elections are a bit more complicated, and yet, with the exception of two states, earning state by state Electoral College votes rests on getting more votes than the other candidate in each state.

In America's two-party political system, general elections present the voters a binary choice. The candidates' goal during a campaign is to woo a majority to vote for them. This can be approached with different tactics, but the object is both clear and simple: divide the electorate between two camps.

A time-honored tactic is to make it a personality contest. In elections for some offices, this is the only viable approach. An election for the proverbial dog-catcher is illustrative. It's probably safe to say that catching stray dogs is not a partisan issue. There is little in the way of ideology, issues or approaches that drive the act of dog-catching. About all that is left is for each candidate to appear more popular, which frequently means painting the other candidate as ugly, stupid or corrupt.

Personality contests will always be part of any election campaign. But as the stakes get higher, involving specific policies, more money and greater political power, the quest to divide voters into one camp or the other becomes more intense. Election campaigns are no-holds-barred events. The ends, getting elected, justify using any means. Other than some rather easily skirted rules limiting campaign contributions, anything goes to divide the electorate, to incite potential supporters to get to the poles and to discourage non-supporters.

This would be a straight forward game if national and even high state-level office elections revolved around one set of policies versus another, one set of choices versus another, or one set of governing principles versus another. But, as the preceding essay explained, this is not the case. The contest is being played on two different fields. The Republican's focus is on governing principles whereas the Democrat's focus is on governing. This would seem to be a clear distinction that would be a basis for dividing the electorate and then try to attract a sufficient number of swing voters to one side or the other. It's not that simple.

Earlier, common American values were described. They have been built on the bedrock of what were categorized as legacy values which have animated America's unique culture for over two centuries. They include effective and responsive government operating within defined boundaries, equality of opportunity, free enterprise, practicality, directness and honesty and caring for the community. As the industrial revolution transformed the country, Americans adopted modern values, which grew out of the need to protect legacy values in a modernizing, industrial society. Some may say that they were the result of new and better governing, and an appropriate exercise of central government authority, but that misreads the genesis of these values and revises the history. The modern values include regulated monopolies and anti-trust, regulated financial markets, progressive income taxation, Social Security, Medicare and unemployment insurance. These grew out of a widely popular call for them, with the people demanding that their representative government act, even so far as supporting an amendment to the Constitution to authorize the income tax. With a swelling immigrant population in the early 1900's, the electorate demanded changes in immigration laws. As the environmental consequences of unregulated industry became evident, the people supported government regulation to protect the countryside and their communities. These changes affected what the government should do, but they never rejected the overarching governing principles that are broadly supported, if not cherished.

Dividing the electorate by making the case that it is necessary to pursue additional governing action that is inconsistent with traditional governing principles is a hard sell. The justification must be convincingly phrased as an appropriate evolution of American values and governing principles. Here is an extract from the 2008 Democratic Party Platform that points to this.

> We believe that each succeeding generation should have the opportunity, through hard work, service and sacrifice, to enjoy a brighter future than the last. … A people that prizes candor, accountability, and fairness insist that a government of the people must level with them and champion the interests of all American families. A land of historic resourcefulness has lost its patience with elected officials who have failed to lead.

That is an affirmation of American values that can, and in 2008 actually did, resonate with a significant majority of the electorate. The themes from that year's platform animated the campaign and inspired a majority of the voters.

Over the next two years, as policies were implemented that seemed inconsistent with the campaign rhetoric, some voters took notice. Perhaps more importantly, some began to sense that the new administration's methods of governing didn't conform to what had been the norms that reflected American values. It was dismissive of alternative viewpoints. It was too certain that its ideas were right. In some instances, it even seemed to deny obvious facts and to twist reality. It promoted moving decisions and control of more and more to Washington DC where voices of experts and academics were the only ones heard. It seemed to defy common sense. A number of the voters grew increasingly skeptical of the administration's sincerity and intentions.

Unexpectedly, the Democratic Party lost control of the House of Representatives in 2010. Undeterred, the administration continued to advance its agenda even though losing the House delayed enacting the most ambitious policies. It pushed on as many fronts as possible, aided by a partisan media that glossed over or failed to report problems and exaggerated positive developments.

Instinctively, the administration knew that a candidate and a political party had to appeal to the electorate's legitimate values and then suggest ways that their approach to governing would enhance them. But they were at an impasse. The governing principles supporting their agenda were not those that most Americans supported. The Democratic Party was convinced it didn't matter. Eventually, they would win over a majority of the electorate to their way of thinking. Their fellow partisans controlled the American Story – the illusion of America that filled American television screens and newspapers and the one that they earnestly believed was the true reflection of America. To win back the House, they would continue the group-focused politicking that had seemingly served the Democratic Party well in the recent past. They went after the parts and increasingly offered faint praise for the whole. It seemed to work. In 2012, President Obama won a second term and Democrats gained seats in the Senate. The election results convinced party leaders that group-centered campaigning would overcome the 2010 setback in the 2014 cycle.

Despite indications that Republican turnout and enthusiasm were increasing, and that Independent voters were swinging toward Republicans, few Democrats paid attention to the trends. They seemed convinced of several things. America was becoming more balkanized, so encouraging more would allow them to target groups with better campaign messages. Further, the increased balkanization would continue to shrink the relative number of Republican voters. After four years of continued electoral success (the 2010 elections being rationalized away), and four years of near-universal media affirmation, they were convinced that a growing American majority eagerly supported the Democratic agenda. On this basis, the Democratic Party not only renewed its campaign marketing on groups and divisive issues. It no longer devoted much effort to try to appeal to Americans in general. Perhaps most importantly, remaining convinced that their values had supplanted American values, it touted them openly, essentially scolding reluctant voters into accepting them. It didn't resonate with many Americans. Sixteen Senate seats changed party hands in the 2014 election, and the Republicans took control.

By the 2016 campaign, it was evident that the two political party platforms shared little in common. The Republican one remained wedded to American values. The Democratic platform left the important ones out. It went a step further by ascribing to the people of the United States values and principles that were, for lack of a better description, un-American. It painted America as a flawed country that had to be repaired[11]. The voters noticed. An electoral majority voted for the sole political party that represented their values and reflected the real America they knew.

Although it is an interesting question how a bulk of the electorate saw past the media presentation of the American Story, it is not relevant to address it here. But it is illustrative of the mindset and thinking of the small but overwhelmingly powerful cadre of producers and publishers that control the media. Cloistered like-minded thinkers, they believe their own reality, incapable of even considering that an alternative reality exists for the majority of Americans.

The divide in America is a political and media construct; it isn't real. America's majority isn't silent, per se. It simply doesn't have a voice. It isn't heard on most television newscasts and it can't be read on the pages of most newspapers. All it has is the outlet of elections to give it an airing.

In an earlier chapter, it was posited that modes of thinking can affect relationships, be they interpersonal or societal. They can also influence feelings and opinions. Even more significantly, some modes can inhibit critical thinking. They can cajole some to believe that they are deliberately thinking things through when in fact they stifle clear-eyed looking at reality and discourage skeptical assessment of actual conditions. The flip side of this is that uncritical thinking, comparative thinking in particular, tends toward the surreal and entertains wishful thinking. It can lead some such thinkers to accept explanations or ideas that defy common sense, let alone stand up to critical thinking.

Modes of thinking, of course, are far from the only determinant of an election's outcome. They are, however, one filter through which political campaign rhetoric must pass. It seems evident from current election trends that many American voters don't share the same filter as their teachers, the professors and those who produce The American Story.

Conclusion

I hope I have convinced you that the areas where Americans' opinions diverge are at the margins of the values that they share. I also hope you don't think that I have tried to connect an effect (a divided America), with a cause (wayward schooling, the media). It is actually the obverse. There is no cause – because there is no effect. Americans are basically not divided, let alone at loggerheads. They share many more beliefs and values than we are told.

Vibrant America is a kind of living, complex, multi-dimensional organism, a chaotic mix of communities that are beyond elementary description. Trying to capture it in journalistic criteria by presenting 'both sides' does, in fact, denigrate its complicated character, reducing it to an overly simplistic red and blue when the various shades in between are more to the point. Your house doesn't have two sides. It has four, and six, if we add the foundation and the roof. And that is just one house. All of American society really has no sides at all.

You need to look at your fellow citizens as incredibly varied, like the flora in the fields or the stars in the sky. Wedging them into groups not only doesn't aid comprehension, it precludes it. America is not what you read in your local paper. It may tell you of events in your local community and neighborhood. It can't begin to explain what is happening across your entire city, let alone the whole country. And it certainly can't tell you why things are occurring, other than simple events like house fires and tax increases. America is not what you see on television. These are but brief video versions of tiny pieces of America, brought to you by a wisp of people who make a living by keeping you entertained. Americans are not the people you see in films. They are stereotypes, caricatures, even cartoons (sometimes literally!) of what a cloistered small group chooses to portray.

Americans are not comfortable with the divisiveness that comes calling each election season. Every politician needs a majority of the votes cast. The goal of attracting it justifies most any means. They'll do anything to make the sale. Unfortunately, in so doing, they paint things red and blue when in fact the terrain is a palette of colors, if not a Monet scene of shades.

The dividers are the party partisans. Partisans are fine people. But we are all fine people, aren't we? Their failing, too often, is that their learned way of thinking has convinced them that since they are fine, and you disagree with them, that you are not fine. That compared to them, you are uneducated, close-minded, deficient, heartless or worse. Remember, comparative thinkers on either side of the aisle first see things through a binary lens.

When meeting new people in a social setting, sometimes the question of one's political affiliation comes up. Some will proudly proclaim themselves to be Democrats or Republicans. A good many will identify as independents. Here's what I have tried lately. I say, "I am a local Democrat, a state non-partisan and a federal Republican."

It makes people think and it is rare that I get an instant reaction. Some people look away, pondering. Others squint, analyzing. A frequent response is, "that's interesting." A refreshingly frequent reply is, "can I borrow that?" It's also remarkable how many simply accept my statement without asking for an explanation. If they do seek clarification, I describe it this way. I believe in an active, well resourced local government that provides the civilizing framework, safety protections and environmental needs of the community. I believe in a state government that appropriately balances the overall needs of the commonwealth as a whole with the rights and privileges of its citizens in a fiscally responsible way. And I believe in a Constitutionally-mandated limited federal government that fulfills its core responsibilities to serve the interests of the people and the states. In short, I am an American.

It is stunning, in a way, that both Karl Marx and James Madison were seeking the same thing: popular political power. Both sought to devise a system for self-government. Marx called them the masses; Madison, we the people. Marx, as a thirty year old academic theorist suggested one way. Madison gave it much more informed thought. He took into account the complexity of society, the phenomena of cultural trends and the vagaries of human nature. America, now filled with remarkably diverse communities of people from disparate cultures has, for two-plus centuries, fulfilled Madison's view. I believe it is because the American people are principled individuals with common sense.

Always remember that you and the many million American individuals like you are mere spectators to The American Story being told by a very few. In the game of America, you are listening to the play-by-play from a voice isolated high above the crowd. Turn off the volume, watch the game and think for yourself. Better yet, go to the stadium, sit with your fellow Americans, spend time with them and watch the game live. Then come to your own conclusions.

And trust your common sense.

Afterword: One Vantage Point

These chapters are the product of someone who's covered a lot of ground. A large part of the territory was my experiences as an officer on nuclear attack submarines. Most people haven't a clue about modern submarines. They imagine World War II diesel boats. Modern submarines are, in fact, marvelous self-contained mini-planets kept alive by the sailors within them.

A modern nuclear submarine has a crew of about 120. I'll generalize to keep it simple, so veterans and military historians bear with me. Twelve of them are officers, college graduates who then complete nuclear and submarine warfare training. The other 108 are enlisted, primarily high school graduates, and the product of an intensive and strict technical training pipeline run by the Navy. Taken in at the age of eighteen to twenty-something, they become tradesmen, technically competent in their field. They are electricians, sonarmen, navigators, radiomen, torpedomen, machinist mates (who maintain turbines, AC units, gears, pumps, pipes and valves), electricians, electronic technicians (who can operate and maintain the control systems), and the reactor operators (who learn the nuclear physics governing a submarine's reactor, how to control it, and educated on what to do should things go wrong). A few become engineering laboratory technicians (who maintain the chemistry of fluid systems and monitor the radiation shielding). There are a handful of others, including yeomen (administrators and record keepers) and cooks (everything is prepared from scratch because space constraints limit stores to basic ingredients). There is but one corpsman, the sole crewmember trained in medicine, capable of surgically removing a burst appendix, stitching wounds or setting broken limbs, treating unusual maladies and even repairing broken teeth or lost fillings, while also responsible for maintaining auditable records of the radiation exposure of every crewman, and even visitors.

Each of them has secondary duties. Everyone is a trained fire-fighter, even, and especially, the cooks, since a kitchen deep-fat fryer fire could lead to disaster. Some are trained as divers and rescue swimmers, as armed security forces, as explosive handlers, even as specialists in arcane, highly-classified fields. When the submarine goes into action, all hands play a role. Off-watch machinist mates help load torpedoes or missiles; some sonarmen join damage control teams, ready to patch ruptured pipes or fight fires. Almost every watch station is double-manned, ready to respond to emergencies. At battle-stations, the control room, the fighting station, is filled with extras to help track the enemy targets. Even something as routine as entering a port is an all-hands event, with extra lookouts, armed sentries and seamen topside to bring on tugs and handle lines alongside the pier. Everyone on board is highly trained, valued, and trusted. Most importantly, each is a team player, selflessly devoted to one another.

These men come from all parts of the country and from varied backgrounds. (It's now women, too, but only until fairly recently. In my time, it was only men.) The twelve college graduates rely on the 108 who aren't. Of the twelve officers, only two, the Captain and the Executive Officer, actually set the tone and determine the course. The other college graduates are granted some of the Captain's authority to carry out his orders and keep watch from the control room or in the engineroom. The rest make everything work. What draws them together, and keeps them on point, is mutual trust and respect. It's a magnificent thing.

On top of all that, they are bound by another idea: a fierce, unblinking acceptance of reality. It is the reality of an often cruel ocean and its crushing depths and the unrelenting determination of any enemy to find their boat and sink it. There are no wounded in an anti-submarine battle; the crew either lives or dies, together. There is no room for hopeful thinking. There is no place for skirting the ocean's malevolence when it is so inclined. There is no tolerance for rosy reports that this system is mostly okay, or that piece of vital equipment will probably perform its function when needed. Mistakes and errors are expected, but it doesn't mean they are treated kindly, lest they lose value as a means to learn for all and to educate those who make them. Instead, their inevitability is constantly guarded against by the team through open-eyed inspection and second-checking of everything.

Interestingly, this does not suppress the men's spirits. It does not limit artistic expression or individual interests. In a way, they become keener within the realm of the real world, not as a substitute for it. Reading Moby Dick when far at sea provides an appreciation for the artistry of the words that can never be found in a college dormitory. Listening to a trio playing and singing against the background of machinery noise giving life and power to a submarine makes the musical performance alive and uplifting. Watching hands bring life and color with crayons to scraps of paper and then mold them into a supernatural flower delivers an artistry that belies the relevance of the same work displayed in an art gallery.

It makes you realize that ordinary Americans fresh out of high school are more than capable of running any enterprise, even one as complex and demanding as a nuclear powered submarine. It makes you see that a rigorous education program far from any college campus can empower individuals to join with others and achieve success. It makes you question the popular notion that a college education is really that important after all.

Notes

1.
Counting and categorizing people by what they do is difficult and the tabulation is far from simple. The American census initially was a count of people to determine the population of each state for the purpose of apportioning representatives to the House of Representatives. The North American Industry Classification System (NAICS) is used to compile data on private enterprises in order to understand the business economy. Other agencies count things to analyze trends or formulate policy, such as the National Center for Education Statistics. There is probably no category that highlights the arbitrary way that counting is done than agriculture. By NAICS accounting (looking at business firms), agriculture employs 160K people. The Bureau of Labor Statistics counts 1.1M people working in agriculture. The US Department of Agriculture's census counts about 3.2M farmers. Putting aside Mark Twain's famous dictum that there are lies, damn lies, and statistics, the important point is that, like every assertion made anywhere, it needs to be considered in context, and thoughtfully. Even something as simple as tabulating a head count. So, how many farmers are there in the United States? Well, as annoying as it may be, the answer is, it depends. In this instance, in the context of seeing what your fellow citizens do with their lives (my purpose), I'll assert the USDA number of about 3.2M. Farms don't hire many people – many are managed by a couple (only one counts as employed [BLS], and together they aren't a business [NAICS], plus, they put the kids to work or get help from other family or friends. Many farmers are part-time and have second jobs to pay the bills. But in their mindset and in their outlook, about 3.2M of your fellow citizens consider themselves farmers. Well not just corn growers. The category includes all growers, be they crops, orchards, poultry, pork or beef. They are people who deal with the real world.

The web sites are as follows.
NAICS tables: census.gov
BLS tables: bls.gov
NCES tables: nces.ed.gov

2.
The Values Americans Live By, L. Robert Kohls, executive
Director, The Washington International Center, April, 1984.
Available at
www1.cmc.edu/pages/faculty/alec/extra/American_values.html

3.
An Experiment in the Development of Critical Thinking. Edward M.
Glaser. (Teacher's College, Columbia University, 1941). As cited by
http://www.criticalthinking.org.

4.
The National Center for Education Statistics is found at nces.ed.gov.
The web site contains digests and tables with a wealth of statistics.
The data presented here has come from a number of NCES data
tables.

5.
Men Are From Mars, Women Are From Venus. John Gray. (NY:
Harper Collins). 1992

6.
Various tables, the National Center for Education Statistics.

7.
Historical tables from the National Center for Education Statistics.

8.
From tables on the census and bureau of labor statistics web sites:
census.gov and bls.gov.

9.
The "accuracy" of polls can mean different things. Does or can a
poll of a few thousand or less accurately speak for a broad segment
of the population, or the population as a whole? Is the poll properly
constructed so as to accurately investigate the breadth and depth of
various opinions? Is the poll conducted in such a way that the
answers from respondents can be trusted? These questions point to

the issue of how accurately a poll reflects reality. There is also the issue of the accuracy of polling to predict. This aspect of accuracy is important when launching a marketing campaign for a new or improved product. It is vital to an election campaign. The accuracy of polls in this sense can be validated in a marketing campaign by comparing projected (poll-based) sales and actual sales. Election results sometimes validate the accuracy of pre-election polls. But election results can defy the polls, sometimes spectacularly.
See Polling and the Public. Herbert Asher. (DC: Congressional Quarterly Press) 1992 (2nd edition).

10.
The close relationship between the media and university social studies researchers is in evidence pretty much every day. The media's tendency to highlight a divide in the country is fairly routine as well. Sometimes, it's hilarious. On the front page "Summary of the News" of the Sunday Baltimore Sun was this description of a news article located on page twelve, the "Nation & World" section. "GOD MUGSHOT: What does God look like? Researchers asked people – and came up with a mug shot. Conservatives and liberals have different ideas." (June 17, 2018).
The article ran in other newspapers as well. It delivered this news.

> Liberals imagined God as "more feminine, younger, and more loving," while conservatives have a white guy in mind who was "more powerful," said the researchers.
> "These biases might have stemmed from the type of societies that liberals and conservatives want," said the study's lead author.
> "Past research shows that conservatives are more motivated than liberals to live in a well-ordered society, one that would be regulated by a powerful God. On the other hand, liberals are motivated to live in a tolerant society, which would be better regulated by a loving God."

11.
Here are three passages from the preamble of party platforms.

"We believe that each succeeding generation should have the opportunity, through hard work, service and sacrifice, to enjoy a brighter future than the last."

"The American people do not want government to solve all our problems; we know that personal responsibility, character, imagination, diligence, hard work and faith ultimately determine individual achievement."

"A people that prizes candor, accountability and fairness insists that a government of the people must level with them and champion the interests of all American families."

Guess which platforms contained the passages.
a. The 2016 Republican Party platform.
b. The 2008 Republican Party platform.
c. The 2016 Democratic Party platform.
d. The 2008 Democratic Party platform.

The answer is the same for all three: the 2008 Democratic Party Platform. It is a far cry from that of 2016. The significant difference is that the 2008 platform alluded to shared American values, as the three excerpts illustrate. The values include personal responsibility, an appreciation for hard work, even the need to be honest and direct.

No reference to such values is made in the 2016 platform. The inspiring descriptions from 2008 are gone, replaced by bumper sticker phrases. Two of the phrases quoted above are from the first three paragraphs of the 2008 preamble. The fourth contains only the following encouraging two sentences. "It is time for a change. We can do better."

The second paragraph in 2016 lists accomplishments of the previous eight years. The third is a list of how Americans have been left out and left behind. The fourth and fifth paragraphs are as follows.

"Democrats believe that cooperation is better than conflict, unity is better than division, empowerment is better than resentment, and bridges are better than walls."

"It's a simple but powerful idea: we are stronger together."

Further down, it includes a phrase that implies the belief that American values are no longer good enough. "With this platform, we do not merely seek common ground – we strive to reach higher ground."

Glossary

The summary of Edward Glaser's description of critical thinking
cited in "The American Intellect" makes the point that using accurate
language is a key to thinking critically. I have tried to be precise with
the words used throughout these essays. However, seemingly
accurate words and terms are often used in ambiguous ways in
today's political discourse. I have decided to list many of them here
and provide a precise definition. The list even includes seemingly
simple words, such as equality, freedom and values. The definitions
apply to the United States and are not meant to be universal.

Authoritarian. A regime of command and control by the ruler of the
government wherein the government is fully controlled by the ruler.
In contrast with a totalitarian state, some social and economic
institutions exist outside of government control.

Capitalism. An economic system in which the means of production
and distribution are privately funded, owned and operated under
fully competitive conditions.

Civil Rights. Those rights enumerated in the Constitution, the Bill of
Rights, and the fourteenth and fifteenth amendments to the
Constitution. Civil Rights do not include any rights conferred by
state or local governments.

Common Sense. Ordinary good sense; sound practical knowledge.

Communism. A social system that prohibits all private property. It is
enforced by a governing system that owns and controls the means of
production and distribution, and distributes all goods and services
according to the needs of individuals, as it defines those needs.

Conservative. A political focus on preserving established traditions,
economic systems and institutions.

Critical Thinking. A persistent examination of all relevant evidence
that leads to particular conclusions by recognizing the unstated

assumptions, using accurate language and recognizing the existence or non-existence of relationships.

Democracy. Rule by the people. The word must be used with a descriptor to give it an accurate meaning. Most relevant examples are Direct Democracy, Representative Democracy and Social Democracy.

Direct Democracy. All laws and government actions result from a majority vote by a peoples' congress or plebiscite. It is often referred to as majority rule.

Equality. All human beings are created equal, are to be given equal treatment under all laws, and will have equal rights to life, to liberty and to pursue their self interest. (The American meaning as defined by the American Revolution and emended by American history.)

Fascism. The totalitarian system of government developed in Italy and implemented by Mussolini. The government is ruled by a single dictator who rejects individualism, defines the common good and controls the system of producing and distributing goods and services. It should not be used interchangeably with Nazism.

Fair. Defined uniquely depending on the context.
      Just and honest; impartial; free from discrimination based on race, sex, religion, etc.
      According to the rules.

Federalism. A political system in which governing authority is shared between a central government and state or regional governments as prescribed in a written law.

Freedom. Exemption from the control of some other person or some arbitrary power.

Free Enterprise. An economic system permitting private industry to operate under freely competitive conditions with a minimum of government regulation or control.

Ideology. A holistic view with an accompanying set of beliefs. Herein it is more properly Political Ideology, but the descriptor 'political' is dropped. It is the view as to why and how people should be governed.

Justice. Defined uniquely depending on the context.
   (Equal) Justice. Reward or penalty as deserved, both under the law and in societal norms.
   (State) Justice. Authority and power to uphold what is right, just or lawful.
   (Legal) Justice. To be tried in court with due process and duly punished.
   (Systemic) Justice. Impartiality and fairness while being right or correct.

Liberal Democracy. A system of democratic governance that protects individual human rights through laws designed to protect a majority from overpowering or oppressing a minority.

Liberal. In the American political context, the Merriam-Webster definition: "a person who believes that government should be active in supporting social and political change."

Liberty. Individual ability to choose and act, without compulsion or constraint, that doesn't infringe the liberty of others.

Majority. One plus fifty percent of eligible voters.

Nazism. A common contraction of National Socialism, the style of totalitarianism practiced by dictator Adolf Hitler during his time in power.

Pluralism. A social condition where different racial, ethnic, religious and cultural groups are intermingled geographically. Sometimes used with the descriptor, political; political pluralism is a conflict among interest groups that is (or isn't) resolved politically by bargaining and compromise.

Populism. A political focus to represent the interests, views and tastes of the common people as distinct from the rich and powerful.

Political. Of, relating to or concerned with the making of governmental policy.

Politics. Activity related to winning and holding control of a government.

Politically Correct. Words, terms and speech that conform to the beliefs and opinions of those who believe their world view is moral, irrefutable and to be imposed on others.

Progressive. A person who favors new or modern ideas especially in politics and education.

Social Justice. An amorphous concept of fair and just relations between the individual and society. It is customarily cited when advocating for government policies and programs.

Values. The social principles, goals or standards held or accepted by individuals. Attitudes, behaviors and desires of individuals that reflect the social principles, goals or standards they hold.

Bibliography

All Marketers Tell Stories. Seth Godin. (NY: Penguin Books). 2005.

Animal Farm. George Orwell. 1945

Beyond Liberal and Conservative. William Maddox and Stuart Lilie. (Washington DC: Cato Institute). 1984.

The Communist Manifesto. Forward by A.J.P. Taylor. (Baltimore MD: Penguin) 1967.

Existential Pleasures of Engineering. Samuel Florman (NY: St. Martin's Press). 1976.

An Experiment in the Development of Critical Thinking. Edward M. Glaser. (Teacher's College, Columbia University, 1941). As cited by http://www.criticalthinking.org.

Expert Political Judgment. Philip Tetlock. (NJ: Princeton University Press). 2005

Future Babble. Dan Gardner. (NY: Dutton). 2011.

Gridlock. Why We're In It and How to Get Out. Payne Edwards. (FL: Signalman Press). 2014

Hidden in Plain Sight. Peter Wallison. (NY: Encounter Books). 2015

Hitler's Willing Executioners. Daniel Jonah Goldhagen. (NY: Alfred A. Knopf). 1996.

How to Think. Alan Jacobs. (NY: Currency). 2017.

Men Are From Mars, Women Are From Venus. John Gray. (NY: Harper Collins). 1992

Polling and the Public. Herbert Asher. (DC: Congressional Quarterly Press) 1992 (2nd edition).

Thinking in Bets. Annie Duke (NY: Random House, Penguin Books) 2018

Thinking Fast and Slow. Daniel Kahneman (NY: Farrar, Straus and Giroux) 2011.

The Unconscious Civilization. John Ralston Saul (NY: The Free Press) 1995.

The reader may wonder why the short bibliography that includes books on thinking includes the book, Hitler's Willing Executioners. The short answer is that, at its core, it is about how people can be induced to think. I don't know if the author's explanation that the German culture is inherently anti-Semitic is correct, but I do find his assertion compelling that thinking can infect society widely and drive it in a certain direction, even to committing genocide.